Crescendo Publishing Presents

Instant Insights on...

BUSINESS

How to Create & Build a Successful Beauty Business

Erica Aker

small guides. BIG IMPACT.

Instant Insights On...

How to Create & Build a Successful Beauty Business
By Erica Aker

ISBN: 978-1-944177-33-1 (p)
ISBN: 978-1-944177-34-8 (e)

Crescendo Publishing, LLC
300 Carlsbad Village Drive
Ste. 108A, #443
Carlsbad, California 92008-2999

www.CrescendoPublishing.com
GetPublished@CrescendoPublishing.com

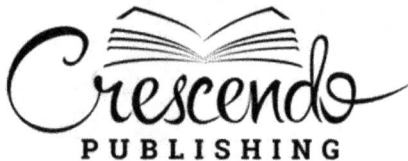

What You'll Learn in this Book

Beauty professionals will learn key principles to attract ideal clients that they enjoy working with, implement new ideas for increased revenue, and find freedom and balance between work and everyday life.

You'll get **Instant Insights** on:

- Using online tools strategically
- Why you should use offline strategies alongside online strategies
- How to be success minded
- Creating an experience your customer will not forget
- The importance of investing in YOU
- Assuming your position—no one needs to crown you
- Being disciplined, consistent, and committed
- How universal laws combined with your efforts will magically open doors for you
- How attracting the right clients gave me my life back
- Attracting clients who value your worth

- Having potential prospects practically begging to get an appointment with you
- Never dealing with a less-than-ideal client again
- Enjoying valuable family and personal time because of the balance created between work and life

A Gift from the Author

Download your FREE accompanying checklist and calendar template to help you stay guided and focused as you build your beauty business for success.

www.EricaAker.com/InstantInsightsBookBonus

Table of Contents

In Dedication.. 1

A Note from Erica 3

Mind Therapy 9

Who Is Your Ideal Client?... 15

Invest in YOU!... 21

Position Yourselfas the Expert!................................ 27

Help Others Get WhatThey Want............................ 33

Dare to Be Different.. 39

Have an Irresistible Presence Online and in Social
Media 45

Planning and Promoting Your Beauty Business 51

Offline Strategies for Increased Revenue...................... 57

Gain and Maintain a Positive Snowball Effect............. 63

About the Author 71

Connect with the Author.. 77

Other Books by this Author 79

Acknowledgements 81

In Dedication

To my husband, friend, and partner, Fernando, for believing in me, supporting my dreams and ideas, and for simply being my number one fan. Words cannot express my love, gratitude, and appreciation for your humor, kindness, and all that you do.

Your encouraging words kept me going during tough times when I felt like throwing in the towel. You've been there for me consistently, and again, thank you and I love you always!

A Note from Erica

Why I want you to succeed in your beauty business and walk in your full potential.

The beauty industry has been around for centuries. Beauty was defined and reinvented throughout different periods of time. In biblical times, references were made about beauty, which consisted of hair, clothing, jewels, and even keeping a healthy body.

We know that beauty was a big deal among the Egyptian women. Even the Renaissance woman had her time in history concerning beauty. If we fast-forward into our time today in the twenty-first century, we still find that beauty practices play a significant role with men and women. Standards of beauty are a staple in our culture, and I do not see them going away anytime soon.

As beauty professionals, we should recognize that beauty services are a necessity in our world. Beauty services have survived through recessions and economic crashes. It's not to say that our industry won't be affected, but people will still find a way to get their beauty services—even if it means coming less often or pulling out the credit card to pay.

This is an awesome opportunity and time to create a successful beauty business practice and build a legacy to leave behind. Sadly, in my years in the beauty industry, I have seen talented designers who are gifted but have no concept on how to handle business matters to keep their business growing. Many are still struggling to merge the two (business and talent) together.

In order to have true success, handling business matters should be first order, then talent. I have known people over the years who weren't as talented as others, but their businesses were thriving more than the talented person. How could this be?

It seems like the talented person who is in demand should be thriving more, right? The reason is that one may be talented and in high demand, but they don't know how to handle business matters or money management. Therefore, a lot of hard work is put into the business, but there is nothing to show for it other than material things such as clothes and cars.

In the long term, clothes and cars will not retire you. When someone reaches seventy years of age and is still trying to work to make ends meet, this is a sad situation. I don't know any beauty professional that wants to still be working at seventy unless it is strictly by choice, not a "have to" situation. Material things decrease in value, and there is no return on the investment. Many of you know that clients come and go. Why not look at your business in the long-term instead of the "right-now" mindset.

In order for any business to be successful, boundaries, sacrifice, and discipline are necessary to sustain longevity and relevance.

It is imperative that you constantly work *on* your business in addition to working *in* your business. You must continuously research and test various techniques to maintain a flow of new business. Having marketing skills is extremely important, but beauty schools do not teach sound marketing skills. Therefore, the beauty professional is left to figure things out on their own.

Statistics tell us that the average working "life span" of a beauty professional is between six and eight years. If they are still struggling and trying to find their way, burnout and frustration set in, and they will ultimately quit the industry altogether and go get a "regular" job that pays pennies, a job where they still aren't fulfilled and happy.

It is my ambition to reach as many beauty professionals as I can to help them see that there is an abundance of money out there. There is no lack with money flowing. Money is a tool that we need to survive and live. The question is, how will this money get handled or invested?

It is also my desire for you to reach such a place in your beauty business that you are no longer bound to working unforgiving hours, missing out on valuable family and personal time. All your efforts should be spent on figuring out how to work smarter, not harder. You were created for a purpose, yes, but enjoying your life is a part of that purpose.

As you dive into this book, it is my desire that you read it with an open mind. Imagine yourself growing and going to another level in business by using these practical techniques and principles that are pretty easy to implement.

Turn your mind toward long-term success. Do what it takes to stay focused and on course to have a beauty business that you truly enjoy. Strive to leave your imprint within the beauty market. Never settle for less than you deserve. I believe that you deserve more! You have worked hard to obtain your diplomas, licenses, and certifications. Why stop progressing and going farther—why settle for being mediocre? Make it your goal to achieve more for yourself and your loved ones.

In life we have choices, and opportunities are everywhere if we would only begin looking for them. Oftentimes, they are either right in front of us, or they show up when we make the decision to just "GO." No matter what the obstacle or situation, those that choose to step up and step out are the ones that get the opportunities. I hope this is you.

I wrote this book just for beauty professionals like you that are ready and willing to step into their greatness. The next chapters that you read are guides that can be implemented in your life and your business. They are outlined to help you find clarity, direction, and purpose. These guides could help you find and attract clients that you truly enjoy working with, increase your revenue, and find balance between work and everyday life.

This is why I want you to succeed in your beauty business. You can do it!

Love & Success,
Erica

Mind Therapy

Have you ever found yourself feeling frustrated when it comes to your work, your clients, or your environment?

Have you ever been in a great mood before arriving to work and then suddenly find yourself feeling less than enthused after you've arrived?

You may be in need of some mind therapy exercises.

Many beauty professionals find themselves experiencing these exact feelings, but they don't understand the root cause of these feelings. They will resolve in their mind that it's lack of rest or they are having a blah day.

They know in their heart that they love what they are doing in the beauty industry, but they still feel unfulfilled. Questions will arise such as, "Am I really doing what I love?" or "Am I in the right career field?" If these feelings or unanswered questions go on for too long, many beauty professionals will get burned out and end up hating work or, even worse, quit the beauty industry altogether.

By the time these beauty professionals get to me, they are so frustrated that they see me as their last hope.

After a bit of probing and questioning as I coach them, I find that most beauty professionals have never really thought of their mindset factoring into their frustration. I also find that their mindset is usually not focused on successful thinking. It's more focused on "I've got to get by the best way I know how."

They had given no thought to maintaining a positive mindset as they grew in business. No one ever told them that they could decide who they wanted to work with. No one ever taught them how to work only with people that were in alignment with their core values, the people they truly enjoy working with.

The biggest frustration I hear is that they want to work with people who do not mind paying higher prices. However, they have been stuck with customers who nickel-and-dime them.

After further probing, I found that the beauty professional having a problem with complainers or those lacking funds to afford services that they needed would exhibit the same exact behavior when it came to paying for particular services for themselves, never realizing that you attract what you are. For example, a beauty professional that complains about prices to their distributors or local supply store for products or tools will typically attract clients that complain about prices.

When attempting to attract ideal clients that do not mind paying the listed price, there must be a mindset shift. A great way to begin shifting the mindset is to practice daily mind therapy. This could consist of reading and listening to positive, motivating, and inspirational material. It could also be hanging around people who are optimistic or those that find good even in not-so-good situations.

Let's face it—the world is full of negativity. Turn on the television or radio, and there are negativity, fear, loss of hope, and doubt. Many of the people around the world feed into the negativity and sometimes, unaware, will project the negativity onto others.

Guarding the mind is one of the hardest things to do in today's society. However, it is more important than ever to do so when you desire to have a successful business working with customers who appreciate great service and will pay for it.

When practicing mind therapy on a regular basis, a reprogramming begins to take place. The mind begins to line up with the thought process it's being subjected to. Before long, negativity cannot reside in the same space. What was once seemingly normal will no longer be tolerable. Anything outside this new positive alignment will be rejected. Sadly, in some cases, friends may be lost and certain family members may not understand this new way of living. However, in the long run, it is worth the effort, especially when your old negative clients either leave or line up. If they leave, it only means that they have made room for the ideal client to be able to come and receive services.

Focusing on mind therapy will fill your spirit and soul with good ideas, good people, and peace of mind. Even so, frustration will come periodically. When it does come back, it should not be as effective as it once was in altering the mood. Things you used to tolerate will no longer be an option.

Daily doses of positive thinking have been proven to be an important factor with most successful business people.

Your Instant Insights...

- Practice mind therapy daily to create a positive mindset.

- Pay attention to how your mood and outlook change as you create positive thoughts.

- Notice the abundant flow of creative ideas and positive people that enter your life when practicing mind therapy.

Who Is Your Ideal Client?

Choosing a specific audience to market to has proven to be a little difficult for beauty professionals. The "shiny object syndrome" is a big issue in the beauty industry. Why? For one thing, most beauty professionals are extremely creative. Having the ability to do hair, makeup, and nails is typically a complete package for any woman coming into the salon, so why shouldn't beauty professionals do it all? After all, that's more money for the professional.

The problem is that this is a very broad audience to try to market to. For instance, although a hairstylist may be skilled in several areas, this may be confusing to a consumer. If nails and makeup are being communicated when marketing to her, but her problem is extreme hair breakage, she may perceive the beauty professional as more of an image consultant than one who specializes in healthy hair. Therefore, she does not resonate with the stylist, and this becomes a missed opportunity for a new potential customer for the hair professional.

In my own experience as a hairstylist, in my beginning years, I started out thinking that I should do "everything" and service "everyone." However, I learned very quickly that I could not do everything nor did I want to. The thing is, I did not enjoy performing all services. I did not enjoy doing acrylic nails because of the dust and the smell of products. I was not skilled in makeup because I did not wear a lot of makeup. I never really had an interest to be all glammed up on a daily basis like some of my friends. I did not enjoy doing some hair services such as braids and extensions. I felt that it took too long, and I despised doing them.

I did realize, however, that I enjoyed working with real hair and the challenge of transforming damaged hair into healthy hair. That became my focus. Before long I became known as the healthy-hair queen. I noticed my clientele grew and by word of mouth it was communicated that I had "growing hands." Women from all over that were having issues with damaged hair and slow growth sought me out. My business quickly grew, and I became very busy servicing within the parameters of this specific area.

It became easy for me to manage my time because I knew exactly how long it took to service most clients.

I encourage you to evaluate where you currently are in your beauty business. You may be talented in multiple areas, but what one or two areas are you most passionate about? As you get specific in marketing your message around that topic, potential prospects will resonate with that message. If you are passionate about healthy skin but also love makeup, create your marketing message around the importance of having healthy skin while wearing makeup. This message will resonate with those who desire an expert that will take care of their skin as they wear makeup.

It's not to say that you cannot incorporate the other services that you enjoy, but the focus should be on one or two specifics in your marketing message. Once the customer is hooked with the outstanding service she receives, then you can introduce her to your other services if she desires them.

When you begin to specify who your target audience is, the quality of your clientele will improve. When there are prospects lining up at your door wanting you to solve their specific problem, you'll begin to notice that this type of customer does not mind paying a top—but fair—dollar for an expert to service them.

I can guarantee that the customer and the beauty professional both will be happy, satisfied, and at peace when these principles are put into practice. It is a win-win situation for both parties. The beauty professional gets premium, paying clients and enjoys performing the service because she is passionate about it. The customer gets great results when her problem is solved.

Your Instant Insights...

- Identify one to two services that you are passionate about. Explore ideas on how to generate extra income by focusing on services that you truly enjoy providing.

- Tune in and listen for key problems potential prospects are talking about. Present a solution to those problems.

- Notice how people begin to look to you as the expert on solving their problem when you step up and assume the leadership position.

Invest in YOU!

Have you ever heard the phrase "birds of a feather flock together"? I used to laugh at this silly phrase as a teen when my mom would say that she wasn't quite pleased with some of the friends I hung around.

It sounded old-fashioned. Of course I had friends who were a bit more mischievous than I was, but it didn't mean that I participated in the "devilment" (as my grandmother called it). I knew right from wrong, and my values prevented me from indulging. Quite frankly, I was offended when I was accused of "flocking" with the flock when I really wasn't.

It was not until I got older that I really began to understand the message my mother and grandmother were trying to convey. They were really saying, "You attract what you are" in most instances. In all honesty, I have witnessed this to be very true. People tend to hang around others who are like-minded, whether in good behavior, bad behavior, or somewhere in between.

When it comes to business, I have found this to be true as well. Most of the customers that I attract are a lot like me. Of course we have differences, but many of our core values are quite similar. One way this has shown itself significantly is when I decided to invest in myself. As I began to see myself in a more honorable way, my attitude changed for the better. I felt more confident, assured, and smart. I began to find myself in situations where others valued my thoughts and ideas. I realized I needed to invest further in myself to increase my worth and my relevance to others. In doing so, I noticed more and more customers with the same or similar mentality seeking my services.

What does it mean to invest in yourself? It means that you have made a decision to get on a path to better yourself through education, knowledge, and experience by investing time, money, and effort to become an expert in your career field or personal self-development.

Investing in yourself will position you in such a way that you can justify charging your worth with confidence. Many beauty professionals have invested in perfecting their craft but have an issue with customers who undermine their worth. These professionals will conform to the pressure of charging less out of fear of losing clients. This goes back to chapter 2 where we talked about identifying ideal clients and specifically targeting them.

When you invest in yourself and confidently stand up for your own value, the right client will be drawn to that. How is it that one stylist can charge $500 for a full head of extensions and another stylist has complaining clients that barely want to pay $80 for the same service? It is because the stylist that charges $500 knows her worth because of the sacrifice and investments she has made to perfect her skills and knowledge.

She doesn't allow anyone to undermine her worth. If they do, that is not her ideal client. A friend told me of an exact same scenario involving both types of beauty professionals. My friend wears extensions as a protective style only. She needed her hair done and walked into a salon that charged $50 for extensions. Not knowing the difference between this type of salon and one that charged significantly more, she went in.

Very quickly she learned the difference. First, the professionalism was nonexistent. Second, as the young lady proceeded to do her hair, my friend learned that the stylist was not licensed. (In our state, you do not have to be licensed to do extensions.) When the service was complete, it totally looked like an unprofessional did the style. The braid pattern was large and bulky, and because the stylist wasn't licensed, she could not cut and style the hair. My friend had to go somewhere else to have it cut and styled. To make a long story short, she spent more money and still was not pleased with the end result. The whole process was a disaster.

Having learned her lesson, the next time my friend decided to solicit a professionally licensed stylist that was highly recommended. She paid a lot more money for the service; however, she noticed that the experience was totally different from the other salon.

She received top-notch professionalism and service.

Her extensions looked very natural and lay flat with no bulky braids exposing lumps and bumps. Plus, she was able to have it cut and styled in one sitting. My friend felt that the higher price was well worth it and could see why others recommended this stylist.

When you begin to invest in yourself and give tons of value to your customers, they do not have a problem paying. Because of your investment in yourself, you will attract like-minded individuals who do not mind investing in their services as well. The end result is premium, paying clients lining up at your door and handing over their money because their view of you is "she's worth it."

Your Instant Insights...

- Recognize the positive change in attitude as you begin to see value in yourself.
- Invest into that value as you continue to grow and see greater potential within.
- Magically, like-minded individuals will be drawn to you, and your circle will contain good vibes.

Position Yourself as the Expert!

Psychologically, many humans struggle with their real value and oftentimes chase different things to make them feel validated, especially as an "expert" at something. Why is it so hard to admit that you know a thing or two and are qualified to share that information for a price? Giving is great, but it doesn't pay bills. There is a time and place to be a giver, but there is also a time when it's appropriate to stand up and assume position with the knowledge and information you possess for a paid price.

High school graduates are afraid to step into entrepreneurship at a young age because somewhere down the line, someone told them they needed a college degree to get started. Once they get the degree, someone else told them they needed experience. So they start at the bottom, get experience, and work their way up to higher levels. Next, someone tells them that in order to be successful, they need to get further education like a master's degree or a doctorate.

By now, the high school student is in his forties, and he still has the thought of being an entrepreneur, but maybe it's not as strong as when he was younger. Even mentioning the idea to family proved that it was only a pipe dream. They would say, "You have a family and a good job. Why would you want to jeopardize that and start a business with no guarantee that it will work? You know businesses fail in the first five years," and so on and so on. ... The dream of entrepreneurship has now died.

My point here is that we have been indoctrinated to believe that there are only a chosen few who succeed, and we should play it safe and not take risks.

I'm here to tell you that you can take a stand and assume your position in your beauty business on your own. No one needs to crown or validate you. Yes, you should increase your education and always stay current on business matters, but if you have had success as a hairstylist, barber, makeup artist, etc., you probably know a few things about your profession.

If you have a desire to teach others about haircutting, then do that. You do not need to get a cosmetology instructor's license to do that. Your work or certifications and training validate you. I dare you to take a stand and assume your position as the expert in the area that you are passionate about and only continue your education and knowledge through the process to stay current and relevant in your chosen field.

When I decided to step out and become a mentor and coach to other beauty professionals for pay, immediately fear came over me. I questioned myself. *Who was I to charge for something that I'd been giving away for free? Besides, why would someone pay to listen to me? After all, I am a nobody. It would be different if I had a big name, such as Paul Mitchell or Ted Gibson. Maybe I should get a coaching certification to validate me*, I reasoned with myself.

All types of negative thoughts came to my mind that could have easily talked me out of pursuing what I am passionate about doing. It was not until I changed my thought process that I began to see myself as someone who was qualified. I had over twenty years of experience as a licensed stylist, a product-line educator, and a licensed cosmetology instructor, plus I received continuous education to better myself and my business over the years. Why was I waiting for someone to give me the go-ahead when I could just assume my position? The answer is fear. Fear paralyzed me.

Fear is usually the culprit in most cases and keeps us from stepping into our greatness. What fears are holding you back from assuming your position? What can you do to get past those fears? Now is the time for you to assume your position!

Your Instant Insights...

- Humbly recognize your accomplishments and do not downplay your expertise.
- Do not allow negativity and critical talk to stop you; it is part of the process.
- Hold your head high and take position into your rightful place of leadership.

Help Others Get What They Want

Motivational speaker and author Zig Ziglar once said, "You can have everything you want in life, if you will just help enough other people get what they want."

In my journey in the beauty business, I have worked with numerous people, from stylists and makeup artists, to massage therapists and barbers—you name it. What I came to realize in life is that everyone is trying to get somewhere. Some goals and dreams may have been bigger or smaller than others, but for the most part we all want more out of life.

During my journey, I realized that I have helped numerous people get things they wanted. I'm a giver by nature, so giving comes easily to me. I would say that during almost my entire career as a stylist I was helping someone fulfill their dreams. Whether I was offering an encouraging word, putting in legwork for a start-up business, even lending or giving a few dollars here and there, I have always helped any way I could, even when it meant getting stepped on, overlooked, or ripped off. All in all, I did not realize that in all my giving, I would receive payback in return.

When I finally decided to pour into myself with my own dreams and ideas, I reaped what I planted in others. When I began being intentional in my business, opportunities and other people have been right there helping me along the way. I cannot tell you how awesome and blessed I feel when people go out of their way to help me.

When you begin to take part in someone else's dream, you cannot help but receive that in return when you step into your greatness. Magnetically, customers will be drawn to you. It could be through a referral, friends and family promoting you and your business, even coworkers who do not mind helping you get to the next level in business.

Attracting great clients will happen when you are intentional in giving, sharing, and helping others. People will go out of their way to help you get what you want because you have helped others get what they want.

So what is it that you want? Better clients? More money? More time? Those things will come to you, but you must decide to help others along the way if you want others to help you. Helping someone does not mean going into debt or taking on a financial burden for them.

It could simply mean being a cheerleader for a friend who's having doubts about her ability, and she needs a positive influence surrounding her. It could mean lending a helping hand volunteering at a local charity. It might also mean volunteering to provide beauty services to people suffering with an illness, such as cancer. There are numerous opportunities to give and share almost daily. Do you have an elderly neighbor who would appreciate a warm hello when you pass by or who is in need of some light chores being done? Giving is broad, but I encourage you to do it in whatever way you are comfortable and that fits into your mode.

Watch your business as it begins to shift in the direction you would like it to because you have taken the time to give back to others. There is power in operating in the principles of sowing and reaping. When you sow your gifts, talents, and abilities into people or causes that you care about, the universal laws begin to work. You will reap or get back the same when it comes to your life's purpose.

Your Instant Insights...

- See the need to help others, and be willing to lend a helping hand.

- Giving comes in many different forms; find your sweet spot and be led by your inner being.

- When embracing the benefits of giving, begin to think of ways that you could help someone or add a smile to their day.

Dare to Be Different

The "herd mentality"—following the crowd or doing what everyone else is doing instead of following your own path—plagues a lot of beauty professionals and stunts their growth. People tend to copy others when they lack social acceptance.

As humans, we are easily influenced by default. Many do not even recognize that they are mimicking others. Studies have shown that these influences occur or appear in nonverbal behaviors such as emotions and communications. My mom was onto something when she warned us in childhood to watch who we surrounded ourselves with and the company we kept. Parents know how easily influenced teens can sometimes be.

It's no different in our beauty businesses. The power of influence is real. Again, I have seen this behavioral pattern more often than not in my twenty-plus years in business working with beauty professionals from all walks of life.

Let me give you a few examples. Remember when the real estate industry and economy crashed in 2008? There was tremendous devastation; people lost houses, money, even jobs. The panic became so crazy. I remember beauty professionals slashing prices heavily in order to keep clients coming in the door. I saw this behavior in several areas within my city, Metro Atlanta, Georgia. I had never seen such panic and low prices in the beauty industry in my entire career. Do not get me wrong; financially, I felt the sting of this crash myself. I lost over half my clientele, but what I didn't do was slash my prices like other stylists out of desperation and emotions. Yes, it was very hard some days, sitting and twiddling my thumbs, hoping the phone would ring or a walk-in would come by, but something within me could not follow the crowd on this one. I felt a strong sense to stay rational and not base my decisions on an emotional state.

Fast-forward to today in 2016: the economy has leveled out a good bit. I survived! However, many of my colleagues are still struggling. Why? One reason is that they buckled under pressure and followed the crowd by heavily slashing their prices. Since the crash happened, it has been very difficult for them to raise their prices back up to where they were. For so long they attracted clients who were looking for a discount, and as a result, fear now keeps them from raising prices. They are afraid that their current customers will leave if they do so. An unfortunate cycle has occurred by following the herd mentality. I once heard someone say, "If everyone is doing the same thing, then you do the opposite."

Although I took a hit just like everyone else did, I remained true to my value and worth. I refused to follow the crowd, which proved to be a wise decision.

Another less extreme example is trends. Remember when certain hairstyles, clothes, or dances became popular during a period of time? Everybody seemed to be wearing the same thing. I know in my years as a stylist I have seen women wearing long hair, short hair, extensions, and natural hair during certain trend periods. At one time, I thought certain styles would never go away. Remember the layered haircut Jennifer Aniston made popular in the 1990s? I could do that haircut with my eyes closed I did it so much.

Again the herd mentality causes people to want to do what everyone else is doing. In business, it's sometimes good to do the opposite of what everyone else is doing. You tend to stand out from the crowd when doing so. As a stylist, I see a lot of other stylists posting pictures of their work on social media. That's all fine and good, but when thousands of other stylists are showcasing their work as well, what makes one better than the other? I say, go the extra mile and do something else that the other thousand stylists are NOT doing.

This may require some thinking and creativity on your part, but it will be well worth the effort if you want to differentiate yourself from everyone else. After giving this some thought, are you also guilty of regularly following the crowd?

What are some creative ways you could do your business differently to attract prospects that will pay you more than if they went to the salon up the street? How can you be different from your coworkers?

Your Instant Insights...

- When recognizing the herd mentality, think back on how you may have been impacted negatively or positively in past experiences.

- Currently, how are you being influenced by the herd mentality? Explore ideas on how you could break free and do things differently.

- Standing out from the crowd takes courage. Think of fun, creative ways to be different in your beauty business.

Have an Irresistible Presence Online and in Social Media

A paradigm shift has happened in the last century. The world that was once dominated by the Industrial Age of warehouses, factories, and industrial plants has shifted and is now dominated by the information age or Information technology (IT). Life as many once knew it has been propelled into a virtual world setting.

Face-to-face interaction and marketing in order to get new business has been surpassed significantly by Internet usage. Potential prospects are now "Googling" to find businesses that can solve their problems. Businesses are now soliciting potential prospects through online outlets.

With all the changes taking place in the world, it has been no different in the beauty industry. We can now virtually show clients how they would look with a different haircut, color, or makeup palette. Being able to see oneself virtually takes away a lot of the guesswork for many beauty professionals and gives the client an ease of mind with trying something new.

Because customers are turning to the Internet more so now than ever before, beauty professionals need to have an online presence like never before. This means that when someone goes to check out a beauty professional to determine if they want to work with them, there should be an online presence made available. This can be done by having social media accounts and websites strategically set up to attract ideal prospects, allowing them to get to know the beauty professional better without having met them.

What do I mean by "strategic"? Your website and social media accounts need to be engaging. They need to be informative and interactive. Nowadays, a business has literally a few seconds to capture the attention of new prospects. If that does not happen, they will click out of your website or scroll right by your social media posts. They will forget you, and it is highly unlikely they will ever return.

This is why you must have a website and social media accounts strategically set up to capture the new prospects' attention immediately.

Following are five suggestions that can be implemented to entice ideal clients to work with you. Remember to make your online presence memorable and irresistible.

Website:

1) **Have an opt-in box giving away a value-based free gift.** The free gift is a great way to encourage someone to give out their name and e-mail in exchange for helpful information that they can use. This will allow you to engage the prospect further with e-mail. Your e-mails are not only for you to promote your business, but they are also to help the prospect get to know, like, and trust you further. You could share tips, updates, and small bits of your personal life that can tie back into the tips that you are sharing.

2) **Pop-ups.** Pop-ups can be displayed after a few seconds if the visitor has not signed up for your e-mail. It is another way to encourage prospects to join your e-mail list. Pop-ups can be annoying, yet they have been proven to be effective in capturing a lead before they exit your website.

Social media:

3) **Engaging and interesting posts with graphics.** The whole idea with social media is to be social. Sharing interesting posts that encourage comments and likes are a great way for prospects to get to know you and like what you do.

4) **Before and after pictures.** Have you ever watched a talk show when they have guests who are in need of a makeover? At the beginning of the show, the guests are introduced. They are usually really frumpy, with old-fashioned clothing and hairstyles. The show says to stay tuned until the end to see the big reveal after the makeover. How many of you have watched to the end just to see the after results?

    The same excitement happens with pictures that are posted with before and after shots. People love to see transformations. When you allow a potential prospect the opportunity to see you take a client that has horrible hair and transform it into a beautiful style, it builds your credibility. They will begin to imagine themselves having a transformation as well. Before and after pics are powerful tools for attracting great clients who will see value in your work.

5) **Videos.** Just like pictures, videos are powerful tools for attracting great prospects to engage and call you for products and services. Because we live in a society where attention spans are at an all-time low, video is very effective in capturing attention. Not only can you capture attention, but a video with you as the star continues to expand upon the know, like, and trust factors. Video gives the prospect an idea of who you are and what your personality is like.

If you are someone that is bubbly and excited, video will allow a prospect to see that. If your personality is low key, video will show your pleasant, low-key style. Your authentic personality will shine and attract the ideal client that feels as if they can relate to your message. Do not try to be someone else. **Be You**!

Strategic websites and social media strategies will have the right clients wanting to work with you. DO NOT half step on this. It is extremely important to place emphasis in this area of business. A great online presence will allow more visibility and ultimately more dollars in your pocket from prospects that will appreciate your gifts and talents.

Your Instant Insights...

- Beauty professionals need an irresistible online presence, and being consistent is key. Pay attention to those who are responding and get feedback.

- Create an irresistible online presence with your website that prospects will feel compelled to continue visiting.

- Attract ideal clients that love what you have to offer, and continue to feed them valuable information so that they become paying clients.

Planning and Promoting Your Beauty Business

Marketing and promoting my beauty business in 2016 is quite different from when I first started out styling hair, fresh out of beauty school in 1992.

Marketing and promoting has been one of the number one complaints amongst beauty professionals. Many have no idea how to market their business because, quite frankly, it just isn't taught in beauty school. Once the student graduates, they are on their own with marketing and promoting their new business. More times than not, many young professionals fail to get enough customers to sustain themselves. Ultimately, this leads to frustration, and they figure they must be in the wrong business. They begin to get discouraged and eventually quit altogether, and the dream they once had in the field of beauty is now a distant memory.

This does not have to be your story. It may take more effort than most are used to, but it is doable.

When I started out in the '90s, people were doing well financially. Getting their hair done was a major priority. Starting out, I relied on walk-ins mainly, fliers, business cards, and word of mouth to build my business. I had such a high return on walk-ins that I didn't need to market any other way. To sustain my business, word-of-mouth referrals have been my number one way to promote myself. However, there are other strategies that can be used to do promotions for increased revenue that are just as important to keeping you busy with new customers as they are to getting current clients in the door more often.

The following strategies should be highlighted on your calendar and implemented every year. Planning out your calendar will enable you to prepare beforehand. This eliminates last-minute projects being thrown together or not done at all because there was no plan in place.

1) **Seasonal promotions**. Each year, winter, spring, summer, and fall are no-brainers. They occur like clockwork. Planning promotions around the seasons are great ways to add to your bottom line. For example, if you do hair or skin care, you

could run promotional deals right before winter by establishing winter regimens to prep and help protect the hair or skin during the harsh winter months.

2) **Holiday promotions**. The holidays are great times to add promotions or discounts. Most people are already in the mood to spend. Christmas is a great time to offer gift certificates and packages. Easter is a great time to promote children's specials. Valentine's Day is a great time to offer packages for hair, makeup, couples massage, nail art, etc.

3) **Scratch-and-dent sales**. Need to move product off the shelf that's been lingering longer than you would like? Perhaps you have some product with damaged packaging. Scratch-and-dent sales are easy ways to get the product moving. Everyone loves a sale!

4) **Birthday and anniversary specials.** Occasions such as birthdays and anniversaries are enticing ways to get clients in the door that had not otherwise thought of coming in. These specials let the client know that you were thinking of them (although you may have a software system setup with a reminder alert). Because those occasions are special, they are likely to say yes.

There are many other ways to incorporate promotions and sales. It will take thought and creativity, but the ideas will come if you sit and think about it. I once ran a promotion that targeted only clients who came every six to eight weeks for hair services. My goal was to get them in the salon every one to two weeks. I wrote up the proposal and sent it out via e-mail. I had two clients who took the offer. With those two clients together, I made a little over $1,000 a year prior to the promotion. Now, by getting creative with my promotions, I make about $3,200 a year with only those two.

You can do the same. Begin to think about what you can offer that would be a win-win for you and the client. Make the promotion irresistible enough that it would be hard to say no. But remember not to heavily discount your value. Discount things that cost you little to no money from your pocket, like adding an extra service that may cost you a bit of time but not necessarily money. Go ahead and be creative!

Your Instant Insights...

- Create a calendar to plan for your promotions and goal setting. Keep your ideas top of mind by writing them down and then transfer them to your calendar as needed.

- Think about promotions that would be yearly no-brainers and schedule them first.

- Implementing promotions that are creative and compelling will draw potential prospects to becoming clients.

Offline Strategies for Increased Revenue

When I ask beauty professionals what offline marketing strategies could be used to increase their revenue, almost immediately they begin imagining standing in a parking lot talking to strangers and handing out fliers—mainly because that was the most marketing education that beauty schools offered students. As a result, marketing has been the number one reason beauty professionals are not walking in their full potential.

In chapter 7 we talked about a few online marketing strategies. In this chapter we focus on a few offline strategies that can be used in conjunction with the online marketing strategies.

Although fliers can still be used, they are not as effective as they were years ago. Potential prospects are more skeptical now and want to see and hear from you before they consider visiting your establishment for products and services.

Marketing today requires that potential prospects know you, then they will determine if they like you, and finally make a decision to trust you. "How can this be done?" you may ask. It will take some creative thinking on your part to figure out what could work for you in your area of business, but below are some suggestions to consider.

Community involvement. Communities are always doing something to get people involved. I know in my community they are always having some type of event in or around town. I once worked in a salon in my community, and the owner was always thinking of how her salon could be involved. For example, we participated in back-to-school events and visited facilities that housed retirees in the area. We constantly participated in events where we could be seen. One thing I always noticed was our salon would always be the only salon participating.

The way to get yourself seen and heard in your area is to participate. How can anyone know you exist if you are never seen?

Community involvement is also an excellent way to get to know other businesses that could partner with you and be a great referral reference and vice versa.

Join the chamber of commerce in your area. The chamber of commerce is a great organization that focuses on business owners and leaders. It's an organization where businesses come together and support one another. The chamber is usually heavily involved in community affairs. The more your business and brand are seen, the more potential business may come your way. The referral system among members is also a good way for your business to stay top of mind.

Networking. Networking opportunities are all around. Research your local area where your potential client may hang out. Search for networking events or Meetup groups, or start your own if you do not find what you are looking for.

Create a referral system with current clients, family, and friends. The best way to get great clients is through referrals. Most likely the potential prospect is already in search of a beauty professional. What better way to find one than through a trusted person that they know? Word of mouth is still king when it comes to offline strategies for finding new business.

Speaking. Speaking can be intimidating to someone that is not used to being in front of a crowd or group. I hear beauty professionals all the time stating their fear of speaking. However, speaking is an excellent way to position yourself as the expert in your field. When people see speakers, they automatically categorize them as experts. If you are one of those that are afraid to speak, there are plenty of organizations that will help you overcome your fear.

I personally recommend the Toastmasters club, a group of people who also have a desire to speak. They follow a curriculum, and it will challenge the speaker to step outside comfort zones in an environment that is safe and nonjudgmental, and that will give pointers and corrective criticism in a very kind manner. Usually you can find a club close to your area, especially if you live near metropolitan areas.

There are many other places or organizations you can join. It may take some brainstorming and creative thinking, but it is possible. There is an abundance of business opportunities out there waiting for you, but you must take the initiative to find them. This means you will have to get out of your comfort zone and begin pounding some pavement to meet people.

Your potential prospects are waiting for an encounter with you. You can do this!

Your Instant Insights...

- Combining offline strategies with online strategies captures potential prospects from both angles. Think of ways to implement both into your beauty business.

- Offline opportunities are all around. Research different ways to get your beauty business out in front of the masses.

- Get creative and think of other offline strategies that you could implement into growing your beauty business.

Gain and Maintain a Positive Snowball Effect

If you believe that you will be successful and you work hard toward that desire on a daily basis, you can make it happen. You can achieve exactly what you set out to do. If you have gotten this far in this book, I know that success is on your mind and in your heart.

I know that many of the ideas presented in this book require change and discipline, but I am so very proud of those that will not be paralyzed by the anxiety that making a change often brings. In life, we can expect change. Some changes will be positive, even fun, while other changes may bring pain or discomfort.

When you apply the principles in this book, it will probably bring discomfort. Try not to view discomfort as a bad thing. Most entrepreneurs that I know personally or have read about have often experienced pain and discomfort while building their businesses. It is a part of the process. You will encounter plenty of hills and valleys, but there will also be plenty of highs during the process. When those "highs" show up, I like to call them "the snowball effect"—a figurative term for a process that often starts off sort of insignificant and builds up or grows into a something much larger.

As a child, do you remember forming small snowballs to throw at your friends? Do you also remember forming that same size snowball into a larger ball when building a snowman? The more snow you added, the bigger the ball became.

In building our beauty businesses, we may experience a very similar process. For example, a student goes into beauty school barely knowing anything, then graduates to the floor to work on real-life clients. Afterwards, there's graduation and finally working in a salon and getting paid. Do you see the gradual building process? As one grows in their beauty business, they are creating a snowball effect. However, after the first few years in the business, that snowball begins to taper off and stop gaining momentum.

Many beauty professionals begin to get complacent and stagnant. They begin to ease into a comfort zone, no longer challenging themselves to grow more. After a while of settling into this process, boredom sets in, and the desire to go further or higher will begin to seem a bit far-fetched to them. Their dreams begin to fade, and desires shut down. Before they realize it, thoughts of elevating themselves are nonexistent. I do not want this to happen to you.

We all have greatness inside us. That greatness is a part of the purpose and plan that you are meant to share with the world. There is no time like the present to begin pulling that greatness into the forefront. When we get out of our own way with the self-doubt and negative talks we have with ourselves, we can truly begin to follow our passions, and our purpose will become clearer than ever before.

In gaining and maintaining a snowball effect, never allow stagnation or complacency to creep into your beauty business. Always stay vigilant in growing your business and yourself.

Ideas to keep yourself motivated:

Write down your ideas as they come to mind. You may act on some of them right away, and you may place some on the shelf for future reference. I love writing down my ideas as they come to me. Oftentimes, I get my best ideas when I'm driving.

Therefore, I keep a notepad in my car door panel to write them down so I don't forget—but I do wait until I've stopped the car! I have made money with random thoughts that come to mind. I like to believe that they are divinely inspired by God.

Attend various types of classes throughout the year. I suggest that your classes not begin and end at a weekend trade show. Trade shows are fun and exciting with a plethora of information and techniques being presented. However, in order to stay continuously motivated, attending classes throughout the year will keep you full and most likely focused. Branch out and take classes outside your normal learning spectrum. Do not limit your classes to only techniques pertaining to your chosen area of beauty.

Have you considered taking business courses or attending seminars and conferences that teach business techniques?

Personal or self-development seminars are pretty interesting also. Oftentimes, this type of learning challenges you in personal areas of your life. I once attended a mindset retreat, and it really opened my eyes with how I was not fully operating in my fullest potential in business because of some major mindset blocks that I had.

If you are spiritual or religious, attending events centered in these areas will also help enlighten or reveal things that may be hindering your progress from deep within on a spiritual level.

Join business mastermind groups. Regularly being around like-minded individuals who are working to up-level their businesses keeps you focused on your business tasks; there is also accountability that will keep you on your toes.

Read, read, read. Know what's going on in current events locally, nationally, and worldwide. I know that listening to some news stories are a waste of time and even depressing. Try to sift through the negative stuff, and focus on things that could potentially affect your business or personal life. By knowing what is going on, you can make wiser decisions. If you need to switch courses or adjust some things, you can do so by staying informed.

Sharpen your skills by practicing. Personally, I would like to become a better speaker, so I practice speaking within smaller settings, such as my church Sunday school class and midweek Bible study class. I once was a color educator in my early years as a stylist. Because I have not focused on color as an educator for a number of years now, I am sharpening my hair color techniques by getting recertified as a color educator so that I can be current with the trends and conduct classes again.

Hopefully, some of these ideas will help keep your momentum going. Do not let it die. It is much harder to get back in the swing of things when it has fizzled out. Remember the snowball effect keeps going and gets bigger.

Again, I know that if you have read this far in this book, you are well on your way. Champions do not give up, and I believe that the champion in you is ready to rise up and proclaim victory!

Your Instant Insights...

- Maintain your momentum by continuously getting feedback and researching ideas on how to stay in front of people.

- Motivation will keep the momentum building in your business; surround yourself with positive vibes to keep it going.

- Notice how maintaining a champion attitude will keep you visualizing a positive outlook on your beauty business!

About the Author

As a child I always knew that I was different. I always had an entrepreneurial mindset. I never liked to do what everyone else was doing. Most kids in high school were hanging out, talking about the latest scoop on who was dating who, or judging whose clothes were the most fashionable. Although my friends were participating in these activities, I found myself being a loner. It was like my body was present, but my mind was on another planet. My favorite pastime was "thinking." Yeah, I know, kind of boring, right? Interestingly, my thoughts were very broad for a kid in high school. I loved to solve riddles that challenged me to think on a deeper level.

As a result, I developed a high level of awareness. I observed things that most people ignore. I could observe situations beyond a surface level and really see what was going on. Some people call it intuitive, instinct, or discernment. Of course, I made mistakes and bad decisions like everyone else, but discernment kept me out of trouble and pushed me toward greatness.

I knew without a doubt that I was supposed to be a hairstylist. I absolutely loved styling hair. As I grew more "mature" as a stylist, I saw my passion for styling hair wasn't as intense as it was when I first started. I yearned for something even more meaningful. I wanted to help others in a different way but still be a part of my beloved beauty industry. I found myself helping other stylists and barbers who were my friends increase their skill set in areas in which they were either weak or where they simply wanted to learn a different technique. For example, one of my barber friends wanted to learn how to do hair color. He had begun getting more women clients when the whole natural-hair wave hit, and as you know, women love color in their hair. Long story short, I coached him on the fundamentals of color. As a result he increased his ticket not only with women's haircuts but also with custom color services.

After several encounters with friends wanting to know how to perform certain techniques, I quickly saw an opportunity to start a new area of business helping beginner and intermediate beauty professionals grow their businesses with not only their budding talents, but also by teaching them how to market those talents.

In my research, I found that many stylists end up quitting because of burnout, frustration, or lack of money within the first five to eight years. If they lasted longer, say twenty years like myself, I found that they were tired of standing behind the chair or being a salon owner. Sadly, they felt stuck; they didn't know how to get out of the rut. The work that they loved so dearly was now unfulfilling.

My desire is to coach and mentor stylists who are up-and-coming or those that need a change.

I remember how I felt when I first started with no direction or goals. I also remember how I felt after twenty years of doing hair and how it was taking a physical toll on my body. Something needed to change quickly. But "what" and even more importantly "how"?

In February 2014, my sister was suffering from a debilitating illness that almost took her life. Because of all the heavy meds, her hair thinned out tremendously. I had to help her somehow. I got with a friend, and we made her a custom-fitted wig. Again my discernment kicked in, and I realized this would be a great business: helping women with chronic illnesses who have had severe hair loss but who find that wigs in beauty stores never fit properly. As a result, my custom cranial hair unit business was created.

I had stumbled upon two business opportunities: mentoring stylists and developing custom wigs. This would get me out from behind the chair where I labored daily while at the same time it would be fulfilling because I'd be giving back my talents by helping others.

If you are a stylist and my story resonates with you, let's chat and see if we are a good fit to work through what may be blocking you!

Benefits of working with me

Here's what my mentees say about me:

- "The guidance you gave me was an answer to my prayers."
- "You helped push me out of my comfort zone."
- "I received knowledge and information no one else has ever shared with me."

My clients benefit from my twenty years of experience as a stylist, entrepreneur, and strong discernment skills. I'm told I'm a good mentor because I bring these skills to the table. I've learned that human behavior is a pattern. No matter who the person is or what career choice they make, everyone faces similar obstacles in life. The difference is how one responds to their situation. Some get stuck and never get past these blocks. My job is to help identify the block and encourage you as you push past those hindrances so that you can stay focused on your vision and goals for success.

I work best with those who are motivated and ready to take a deep look at where they are in their career and where they want to be. I will help you clarify your vision, set specific goals, and challenge you to execute them.

I do not work well with those who are not teachable and open to new ideas. I will challenge you to treat your career like a business and not a hobby. My teaching method is gentle, yet straightforward. My first requirement of a student is a commitment to be responsible.

Erica's Signature Talks for Speaking Engagements:

- "I've Graduated ... Now What? 10 Things I Wish I Had Known before Leaving Beauty School"
- "Are You Contributing to the Hair-Loss Epidemic?"
- "Stand Out & Be Seen: 7 Steps to Find Your Place in a Crowded World"
- "No Longer a Hobby! 3 Key Benefits to Using Your Talents to Make Money"

Connect with the Author

Website:
www.EricaAker.com

Email:
Erica@EricaAker.com

Social Media:
Facebook: www.facebook.com/EricaAker

LinkedIn: www.linkedin.com/in/EricaAker/

Twitter: @EricaAker

Instagram: www.instagram.com/EricaAker

Periscope: @EricaAker

Pinterest: www.pinterest.com/EricaAker

Other Books by this Author

How to Build Momentum in Your Beauty Business: A Quick Start Guide to Building a Business You Absolutely Love, Win Loyal Clients, and Grow Your Income Fast (digital download workbook)

3 Massive Mistakes Beauty Pros Make That Kill Their Income and How You Can Avoid Them (eBook)

Acknowledgements

To my parents, Willie and Annie Hughey, for believing in and trusting my decision to follow my own path of entrepreneurship in the beauty industry and not be led by status quo. I strive daily to continue to make you proud!

To my sister, Audrey, although dealing with a devastating illness, your daily fight to live has inspired me deeply. I now understand that life may shoot some curveballs, but it is how we respond that makes the difference. Thank you for your continuous love and support.

To my big brother, Alfredo, and sister-in-law, Lynell, thank you for your prayers, encouragement, and support. I am so blessed to have you two in my corner.

To my niece and nephews, goddaughter, close friends, and colleagues for supporting me through words and deeds, and simply being present in my life, thank you!

To my pastor and church family of University of Hope Church, I am thankful to have supportive and encouraging people in my life. I am so happy to have been challenged to get out of my comfort zone by a spiritual leader who understands, recognizes, and teaches that applying spiritual principles in our business is the key to success.

About Crescendo Publishing

Crescendo Publishing is a boutique-style, concierge VIP publishing company assisting entrepreneurs with writing, publishing, and promoting their books for the purposes of lead-generation and achieving global platform growth, then monetizing it for even more income opportunities.

Check out some of our latest best-selling AuthorPreneurs at http://CrescendoPublishing. com/new-authors/.

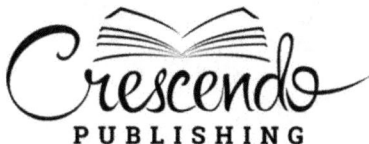

About the Instant Insights™ Book Series

The *Instant Insights™ Book Series* is a fact-only, short-read, book series written by EXPERTS in very specialized categories. These high-value, high-quality books can be produced in ONLY 6-8 weeks, from concept to launch, in BOTH PRINT & eBOOK Formats!

This book series is FOR YOU if:

- You are an expert in your niche or area of specialty

- You want to write a book to position yourself as an expert

- You want YOUR OWN book – NOT a chapter in someone else's book

- You want to have a book to give to people when you're speaking at events or simply networking

- You want to have it available quickly

- You don't have the time to invest in writing a 200-page full book

- You don't have a ton of money to invest in the production of a full book – editing, cover design, interior layout, best-seller promotion

- You don't have a ton of time to invest in finding quality contractors for the production of your book – editing, cover design, interior layout, best-seller promotion

For more information on how you can become an *Instant Insights™* author, visit **www.InstantInsightsBooks.com**